HAL LEONARD *EVEN MORE* EASY POP RHYTHMS
GUITAR METHOD
Supplement to Any Guitar Method

INTRODUCTION

Welcome to *Even More Easy Pop Rhythms*, a collection of 20 pop and rock favorites arranged for easy chord strumming on the guitar. If you're a beginning or intermediate guitarist, you've come to the right place. With the songs in this book, you can practice basic chords and strum patterns – plus learn how to play 20 great tunes!

This book can be used on its own or as a supplement to any guitar method. If you're using it with the *Hal Leonard Guitar Method*, it coordinates with the chords and skills introduced in Book 3. Use the table of contents on page 3 to see what chords each song contains and to determine when you're ready to play a song.

ISBN 978-0-634-04458-8

7777 W. BLUEMOUND RD. P.O. BOX 13819 MILWAUKEE, WI 53213

Visit Hal Leonard Online at
www.halleonard.com

SONG STRUCTURE

The songs in this book have different sections, which may or may not include the following:

Intro
This is usually a short instrumental section that "introduces" the song at the beginning.

Verse
This is one of the main sections of a song and conveys most of the storyline. A song usually has several verses, all with the same music but each with different lyrics.

Chorus
This is often the most memorable section of a song. Unlike the verse, the chorus usually has the same lyrics every time it repeats.

Bridge
This section is a break from the rest of the song, often having a very different chord progression and feel.

Solo
This is an instrumental section, often played over the verse or chorus structure.

Outro
Similar to an intro, this section brings the song to an end.

ENDINGS & REPEATS

Many of the songs have some new symbols that you must understand before playing. Each of these represents a different type of ending.

1st and 2nd Endings
These are indicated by brackets and numbers. The first time through a song section, play the first ending and then repeat. The second time through, skip the first ending, and play through the second ending.

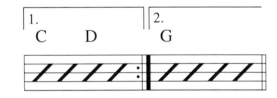

D.S.
This means "Dal Segno" or "from the sign." When you see this abbreviation above the staff, find the sign (𝄋) earlier in the song and resume playing from that point.

al Coda
This means "to the Coda," a concluding section in the song. If you see the words "D.S. al Coda," return to the sign (𝄋) earlier in the song and play until you see the words "To Coda," then skip to the Coda at the end of the song, indicated by the symbol: ⊕.

al Fine
This means "to the end." If you see the words "D.S. al Fine," return to the sign (𝄋) earlier in the song and play until you see the word "Fine."

D.C.
This means "Da Capo" or "from the head." When you see this abbreviation above the staff, return to the beginning (or "head") of the song and resume playing.

CONTENTS

SONG	RECORDING ARTIST	CHORDS	PAGE
Dreams	Fleetwood Mac	Fmaj7, G, Am	4
Good Riddance (Time of Your Life)	Green Day	G, Cadd9, D, Em, C	6
One Love	Bob Marley	B♭, F, E♭, Gm (3-note forms)	8
Otherside	Red Hot Chili Peppers	Am, Em G, F, C	10
Island in the Sun	Weezer	Em, Am, D, G, D5, G5, C5, A5	12
I Won't Back Down	Tom Petty	E5, D5, G5, C5, C, G, D, Em	14
(Smooth As) Tennessee Whiskey	Chris Stapleton	A, Bm	16
Hello	Adele	Em, G, D, C, Bm	18
Thinking Out Loud	Ed Sheeran	D, G, A, Em, Bm	20
Signs	Five Man Electrical Band/Tesla	D, Dsus4, C, G, A, Bm, Cadd9	22
Angie	The Rolling Stones	Am, E7, G, F, C, Dm	24
Give Me One Reason	Tracy Chapman	F♯, B, C♯	26
R.O.C.K. in the U.S.A. (A Salute to 60's Rock)	John Mellencamp	E, A, D, B	28
I'm Yours	Jason Mraz	A, E, F♯m, D, B7	30
Upside Down	Jack Johnson	E, F♯m, A, B, G♯m	32
Crazy Little Thing Called Love	Queen	D, Dsus4, G, C, B♭, E, A, F	34
Across the Universe	The Beatles	D, Bm, F♯m, Em, A7, Gm, A, G	36
I Will	The Beatles	F, Dm, Gm, C7, Am, F7, B♭, G7, C, D♭7	38
Smooth	Santana featuring Rob Thomas	Am, F, E7, Dm7, Bm7(♭5), E, G7, F♯7sus4	40
While My Guitar Gently Weeps	The Beatles	Am, Am/G, D/F♯, F, G, D, E, C, A, C♯m, F♯m, Bm	43
STRUM PATTERNS			46

DREAMS

Fmaj7   G   Am

Words and Music by
Stevie Nicks

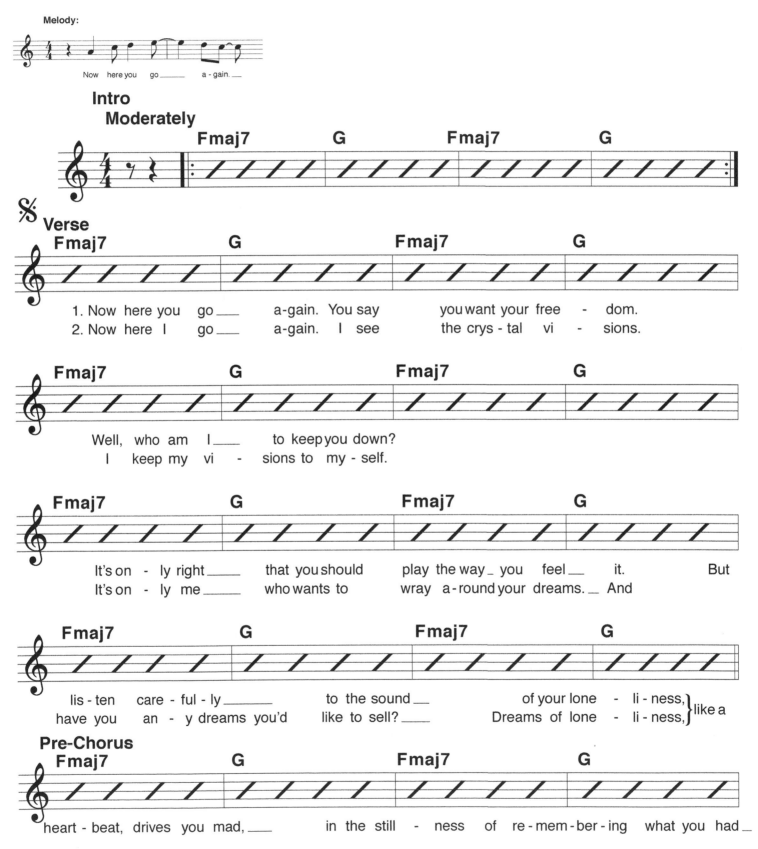

Melody:

Now here you go_____ a - gain._____

Intro
Moderately

Fmaj7 | G | Fmaj7 | G

Verse

Fmaj7 | G | Fmaj7 | G

1. Now here you go_____ a-gain. You say   you want your free - dom.
2. Now here I go_____ a-gain. I see   the crys - tal vi - sions.

Fmaj7 | G | Fmaj7 | G

Well, who am I____   to keep you down?
I keep my vi - sions to my - self.

Fmaj7 | G | Fmaj7 | G

It's on - ly right____   that you should   play the way_ you feel__ it.   But
It's on - ly me____   who wants to   wrap a-round your dreams. _ And

Fmaj7 | G | Fmaj7 | G

lis - ten care - ful - ly_____   to the sound __   of your lone - li - ness,⎫like a
have you an - y dreams you'd   like to sell? ___   Dreams of lone - li - ness,⎭

Pre-Chorus

Fmaj7 | G | Fmaj7 | G

heart - beat, drives you mad, ___   in the still - ness of re - mem - ber - ing what you had__

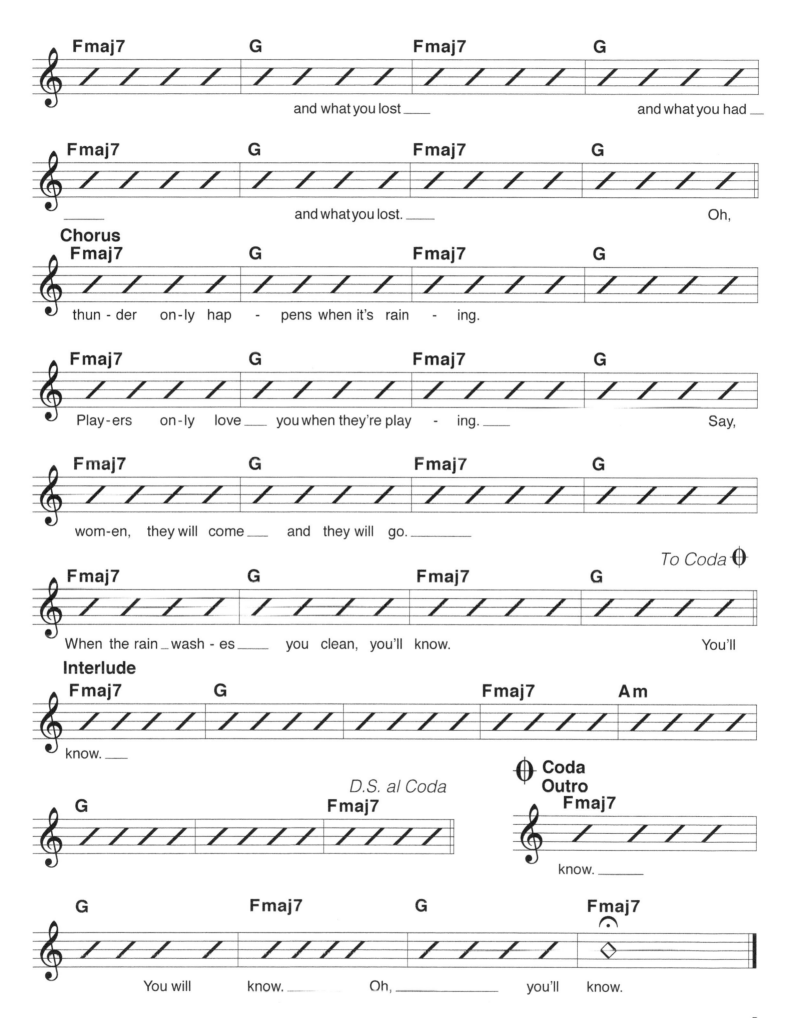

GOOD RIDDANCE
(TIME OF YOUR LIFE)

Words by Billie Joe
Music by Green Day

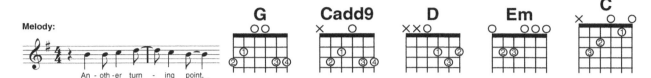

Melody:

An - oth - er turn - ing point,

Intro
Moderately fast

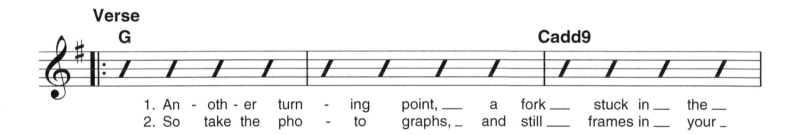

Verse

G

Cadd9

1. An - oth - er turn - ing point, ___ a fork ___ stuck in ___ the ___
2. So take the pho - to graphs, _ and still ___ frames in ___ your _

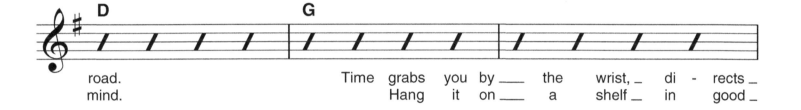

D

G

road. Time grabs you by ___ the wrist, _ di - rects _
mind. Hang it on ___ a shelf _ in good _

Cadd9

D

Em

___ you where to ___ go. So make the best _
___ health and ___ good _ time. Tat - toos of mem -

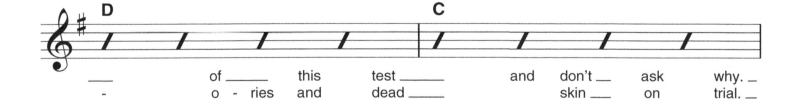

D

C

___ of ___ this test ___ and don't ___ ask why. _
- o - ries and dead ___ skin ___ on trial. _

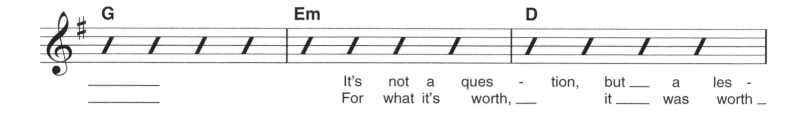

G   Em   D

It's not a ques - tion, but _ a les -
For what it's worth, ___ it ____ was worth _

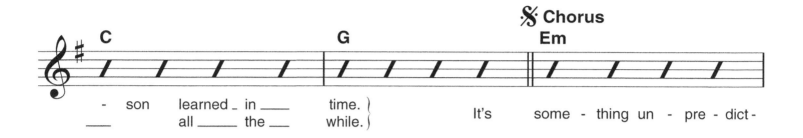

% **Chorus**

C   G   Em

- son learned _ in ___ time.)
___ all ___ the ___ while.)   It's some - thing un - pre - dict -

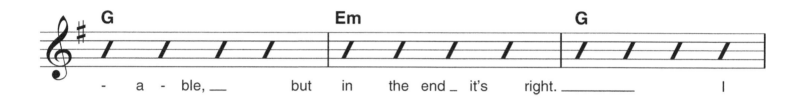

G   Em   G

- a - ble, ___ but in the end _ it's right. _____ I

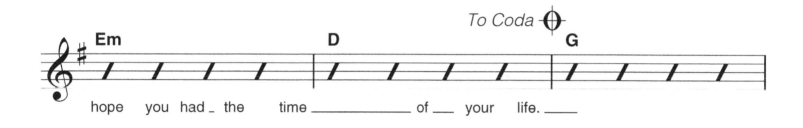

To Coda ⊕

Em   D   G

hope you had _ the time _____ of _ your life. ____

1.

Cadd9   D

2.   *D.S. al Coda*   ⊕ **Coda**

D   G

It's   ___

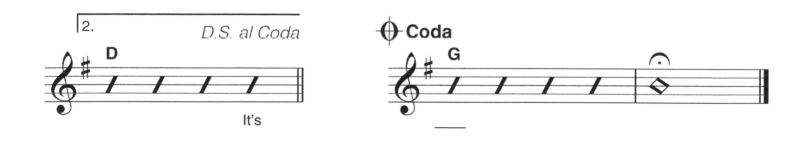

ONE LOVE

Words and Music by
Bob Marley

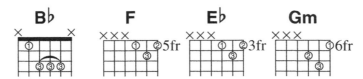

Intro

Moderately slow

Chorus

One love, _____ one heart. _____ Let's get to-geth-er and

feel al-right. __ Hear the chil-dren cry - ing, (One love. __) hear the chil-dren_

cry - ing. (One heart. ___) Say - ing, give thanks and praise to the Lord and I will

feel al-right. ___ Say-ing, let's get to-geth-er and feel al - right, whoa.

Verse

1. Let them all pass all their dir-ty re-marks. There is one ques-tion I'd
2. Let's get to-geth-er to fight this ho-ly Ar-ma-ged-di-on. So when the man comes there will

Otherside

Words and Music by
Anthony Kiedis, Flea,
John Frusciante
and Chad Smith

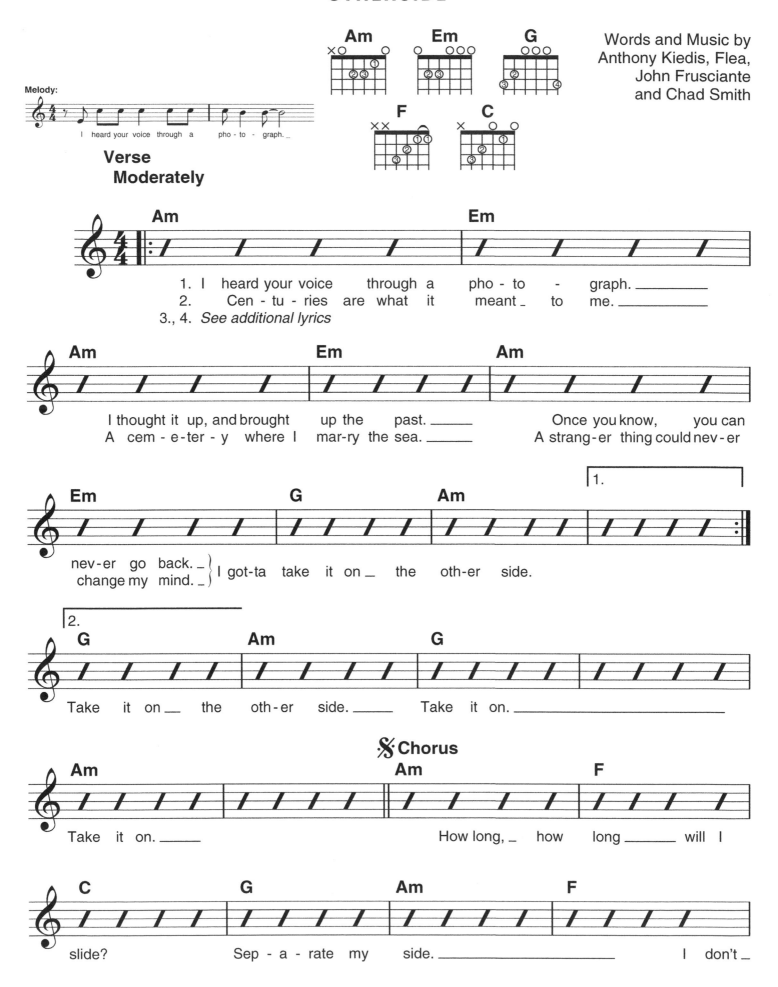

Verse
Moderately

Am / / / / **Em** / / / /
1. I heard your voice through a pho - to - graph. _____
2. Cen - tu - ries are what it meant _ to me. _____
3., 4. *See additional lyrics*

Am / / / / **Em** / / / **Am** / / / /
I thought it up, and brought up the past. _____ Once you know, you can
A cem - e - ter - y where I mar - ry the sea. _____ A strang - er thing could nev - er

Em / / / / **G** / / / **Am** / / / / 1. / / / :
nev - er go back. _ } I got - ta take it on _ the oth - er side.
change my mind. _ }

2.
G / / / / **Am** / / / **G** / / / / / / / /
Take it on _ the oth - er side. _____ Take it on. _____

𝄋 Chorus

Am / / / / **Am** / / / **F** / / / /
Take it on. _____ How long, _ how long _____ will I

C / / / / **G** / / / **Am** / / / **F** / / / /
slide? Sep - a - rate my side. _____ I don't _

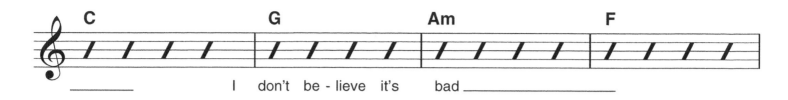

C   G   Am   F

_____ I don't be - lieve it's bad _____

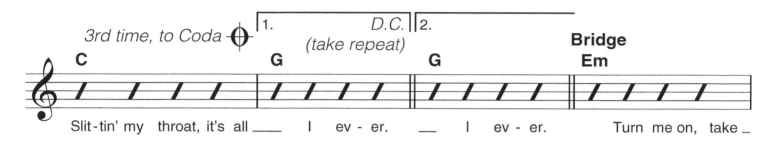

3rd time, to Coda ⊕   1.   D.C.   2.   **Bridge**

         (take repeat)

C   G   G   **Em**

Slit-tin' my throat, it's all ___ I ev - er. __ I ev - er. Turn me on, take _

C

__ me for a hand _ ride.   Burn me out, leave _ me on the oth - er side. _

Em   C

I yell and tell it that it's not my friend. _ I tear it down. I tear it down and then it's

D.S. al Coda   ⊕ **Coda**   **Outro**

         G   Am

born a - gain. _   __ I ev - er had.

F   C   G   Am

Slit-tin' my throat, it's all ____ I ev - er.

Additional Lyrics

3. Pour my life into a paper cup.
   The ashtray's full and I'm spillin' my guts.
   She wants to know, am I still a slut?
   I gotta take it on the other side.

4. A scarlet starlet and she's in my bed.
   A candidate for my soul mate bled.
   Push the trigger and I pull the thread.
   I gotta take it on the other side.

ISLAND IN THE SUN

Words and Music by
Rivers Cuomo

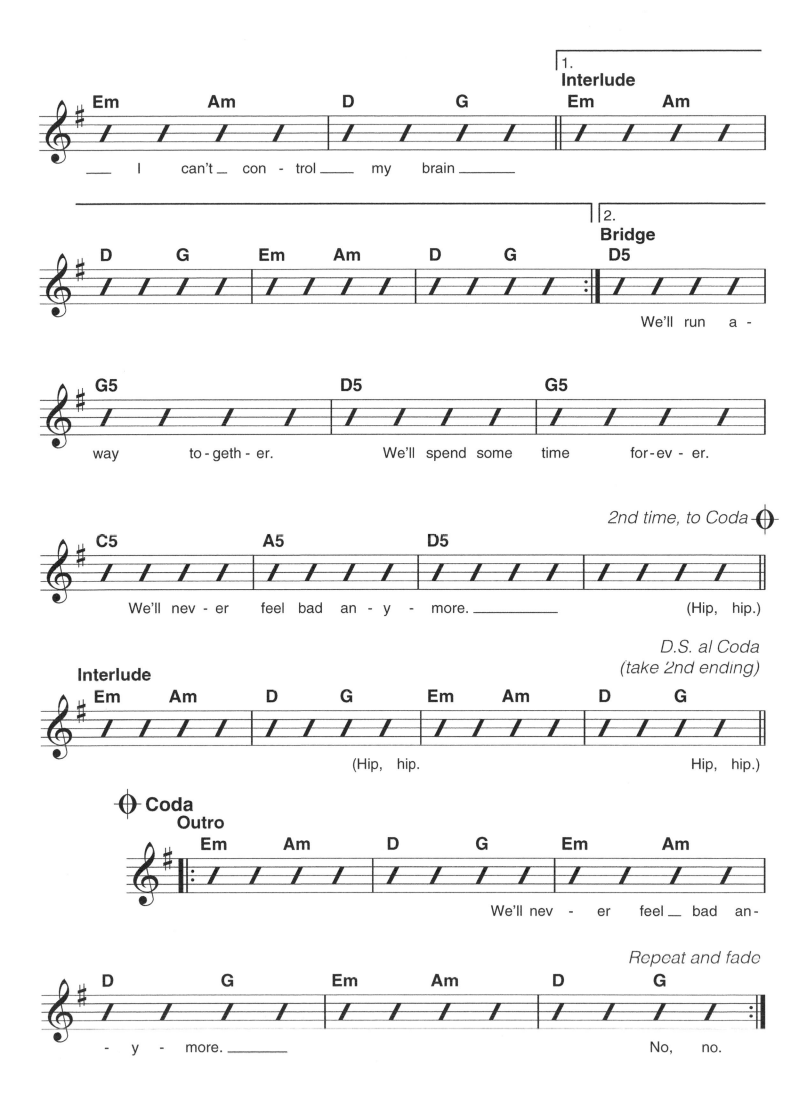

I WON'T BACK DOWN

Words and Music by
Tom Petty and Jeff Lynne

14

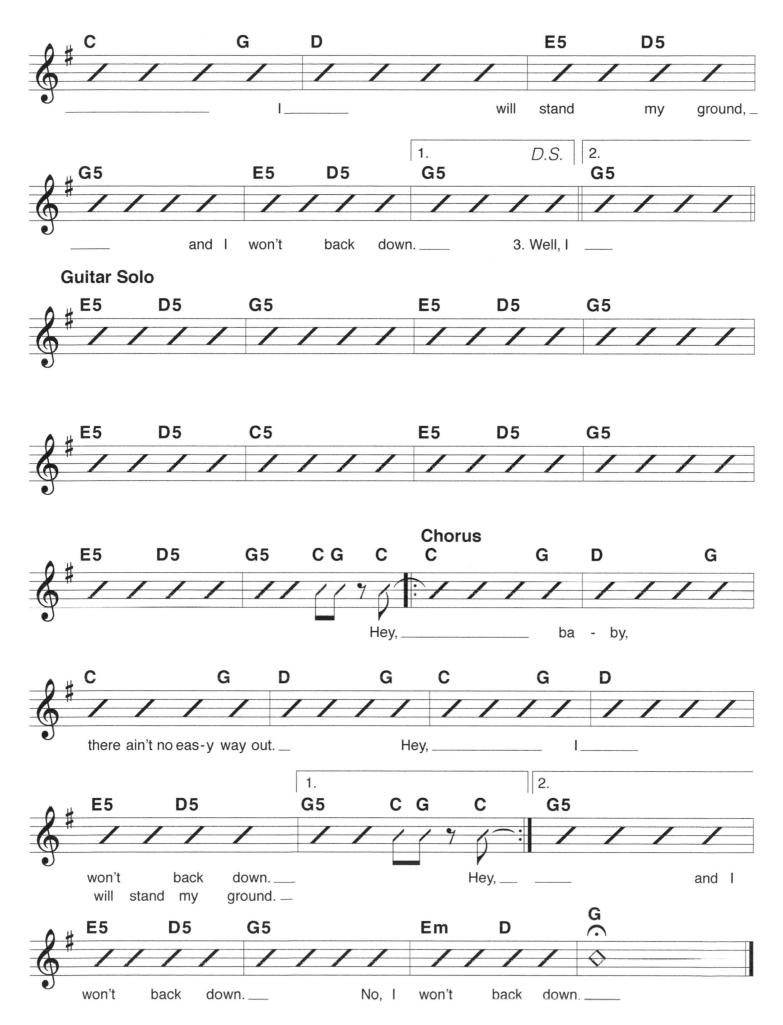

C   G   D   E5   D5

_____ I_____ will stand   my   ground, _

G5   E5   D5 | 1.   *D.S.* | 2.
                                      G5   G5

_____ and I won't back down.____   3. Well, I ____

Guitar Solo

E5   D5   G5   E5   D5   G5

E5   D5   C5   E5   D5   G5

                                          Chorus
E5   D5   G5   C G   C   C   G   D   G

                          Hey, _____ ba - by,

C   G   D   G   C   G   D

there ain't no eas-y way out. __   Hey, _____ I_____

| 1. | 2.
E5   D5   G5   C G   C   G5

won't   back   down.____   and I
will stand my ground. __   Hey, __ ____

E5   D5   G5   Em   D   **G**

won't back down. ___   No, I won't back down. _____

(SMOOTH AS) TENNESSEE WHISKEY

Words and Music by
Dean Dillon and
Linda Hargrove

16

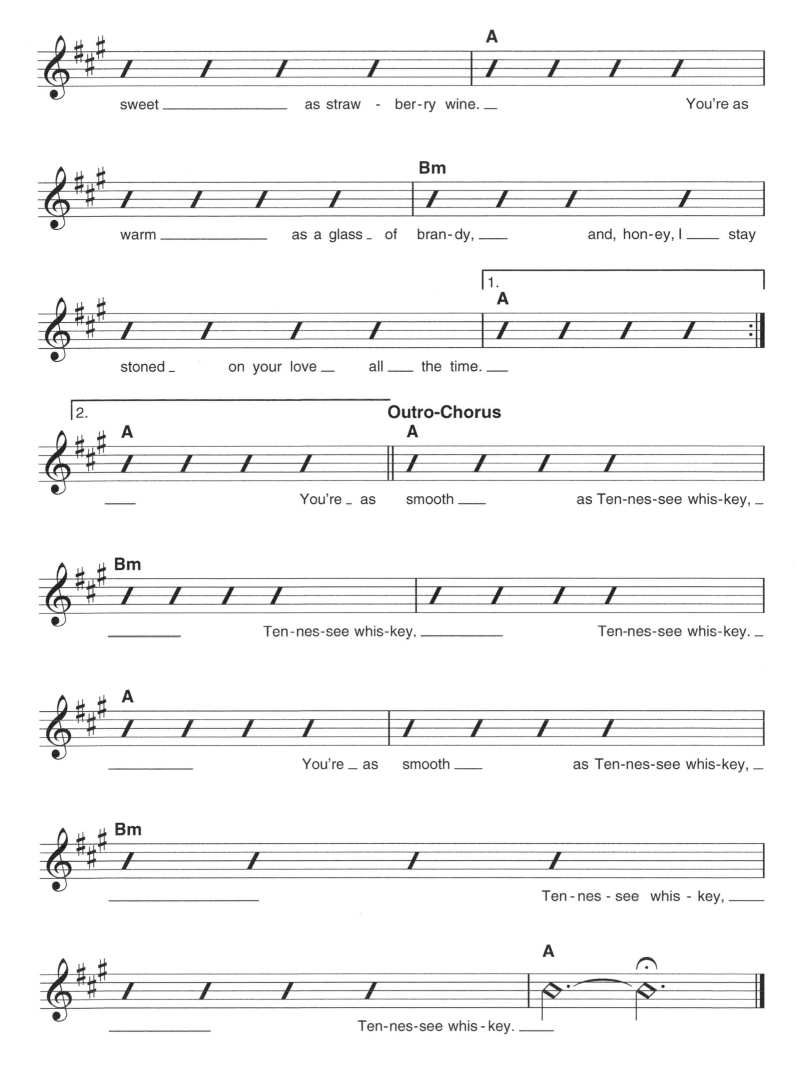

sweet _____ as straw - ber-ry wine. __

You're as

warm _____ as a glass _ of bran-dy, ____

and, hon-ey, I ____ stay

1.

stoned _ on your love _ all __ the time. __

2.

Outro-Chorus

____

You're _ as smooth ____ as Ten-nes-see whis-key, _

_____

Ten-nes-see whis-key, _____

Ten-nes-see whis-key. _

_____

You're _ as smooth ____ as Ten-nes-see whis-key, _

_____

Ten - nes - see whis - key, ____

_____

Ten-nes-see whis-key. _____

Hello

Words and Music by
Adele Adkins and
Greg Kurstin

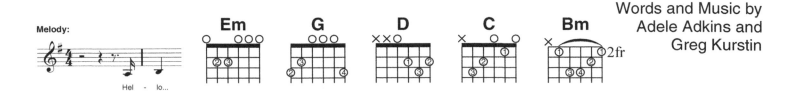

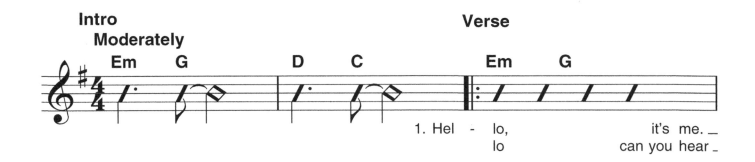

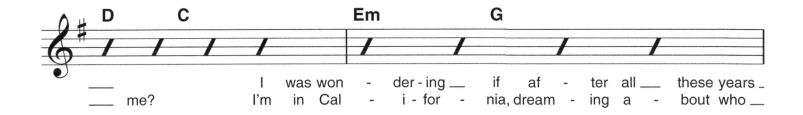

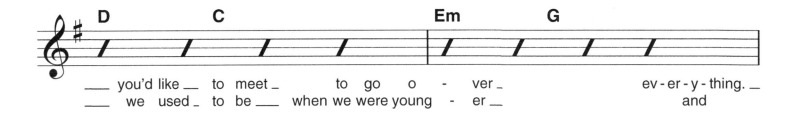

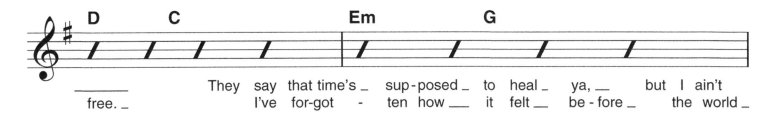

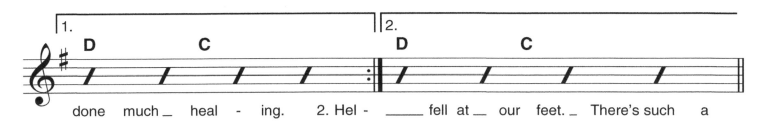

Pre-Chorus

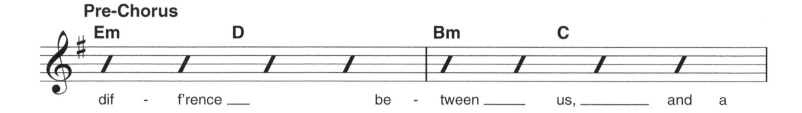

dif - f'rence ___ be - tween ___ us, ___ and a

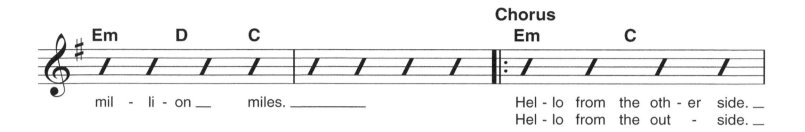

mil - li - on ___ miles. ___

Chorus

Hel - lo from the oth - er side. ___
Hel - lo from the out - side. ___

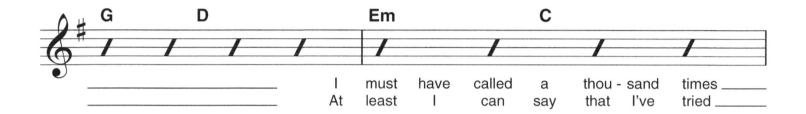

___
I must have called a thou - sand times ___
At least I can say that I've tried ___

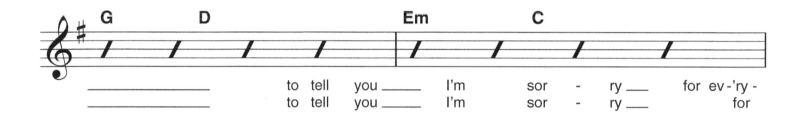

___
to tell you ___ I'm sor - ry ___ for ev - 'ry-
to tell you ___ I'm sor - ry ___ for

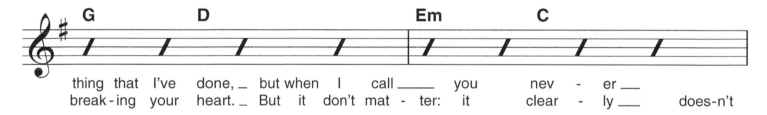

thing that I've done, ___ but when I call ___ you nev - er ___
break - ing your heart. ___ But it don't mat - ter: it clear - ly ___ does-n't

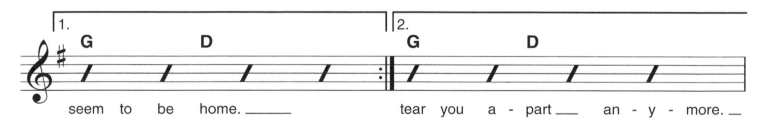

1.   2.

seem to be home. ___   tear you a - part ___ an - y - more. ___

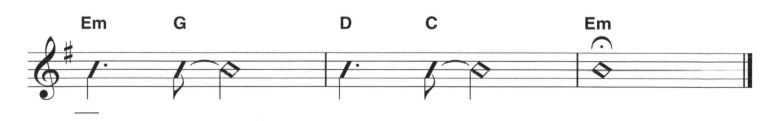

___

19

Thinking Out Loud

Additional Lyrics

3. When my hair's all gone and my memory fades
   And the crowds don't remember my name,
   When my hands don't play the strings the same way,
   I know you will still love me the same.

4. 'Cause honey, your soul could never grow old, it's evergreen.
   And baby, your smile's forever in my mind and memory.

Signs

Words and Music by
Les Emmerson

ANGIE

Words and Music by
Mick Jagger and Keith Richards

GIVE ME ONE REASON

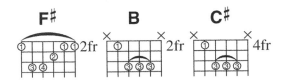

F#   B   C#

Words and Music by
Tracy Chapman

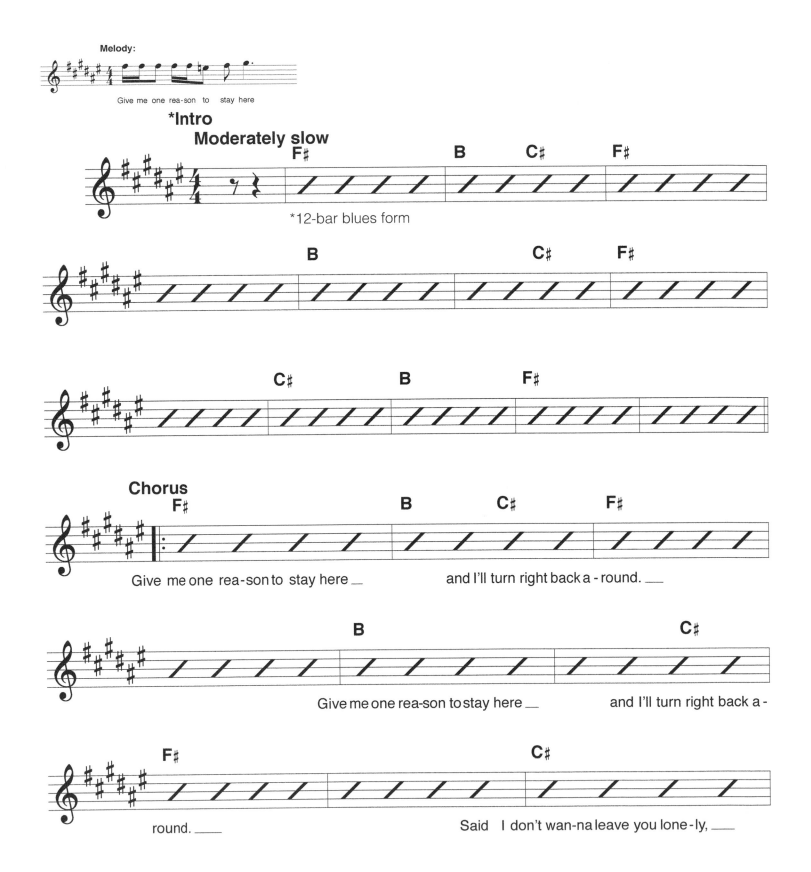

R.O.C.K. IN THE U.S.A.
(A Salute to 60's Rock)

Words and Music by
John Mellencamp

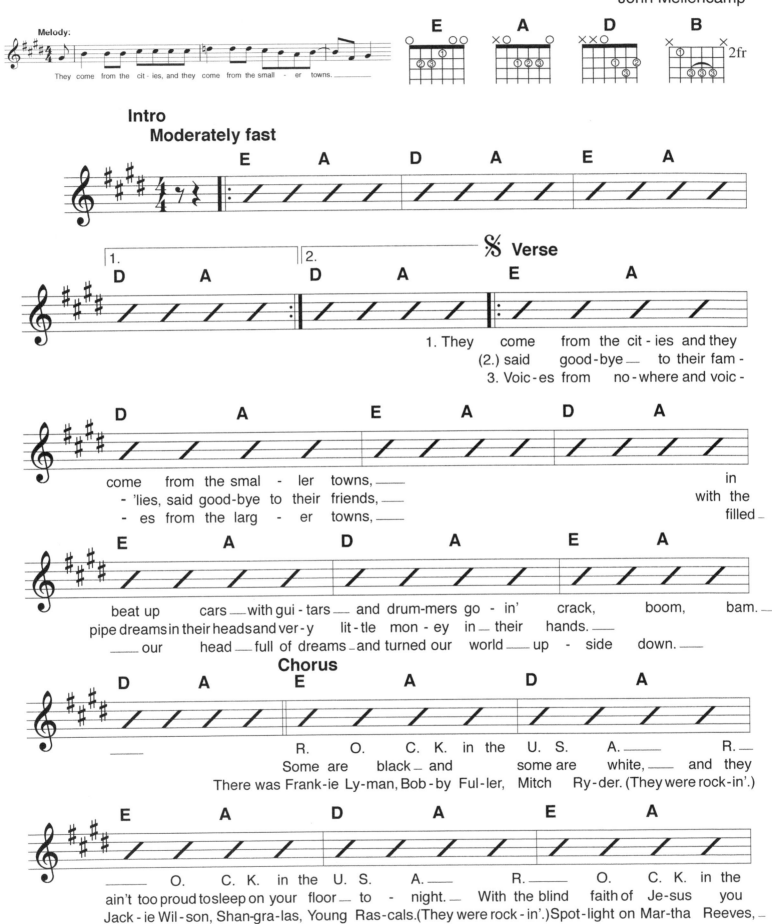

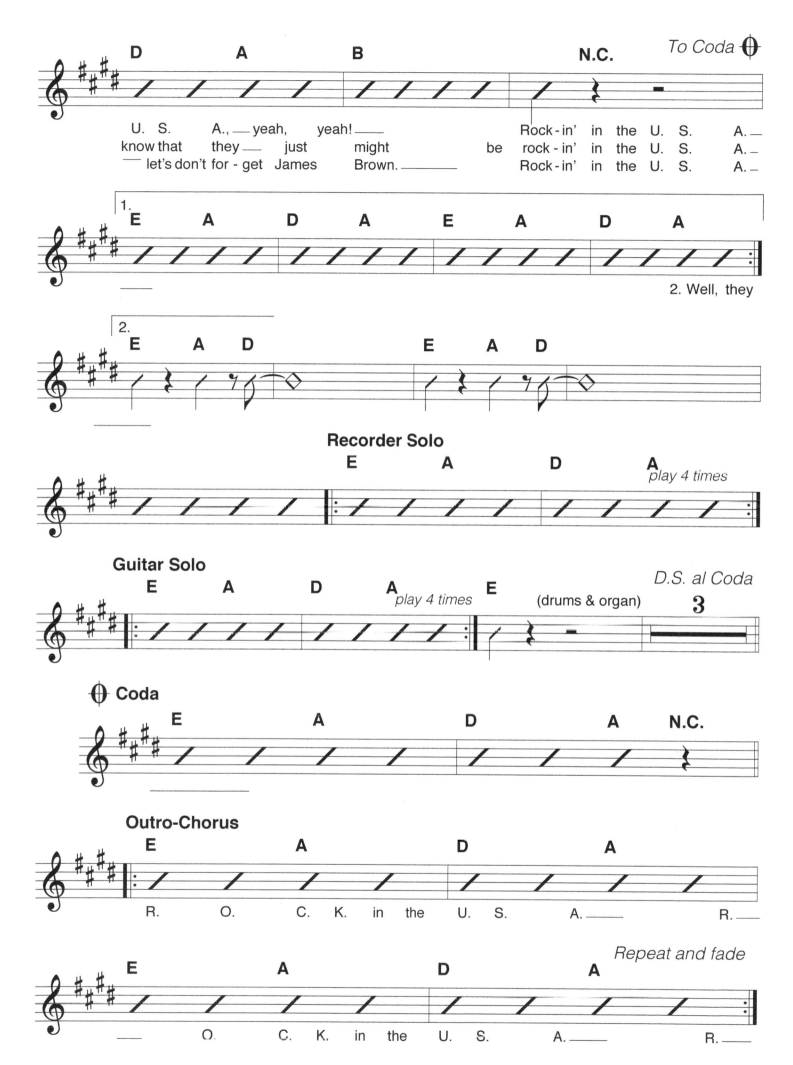

To Coda ⊕

D   A   B   N.C.

U. S. A., — yeah, yeah! —   Rock-in' in the U. S. A. —
know that they — just   might   be rock-in' in the U. S. A. —
— let's don't for-get James   Brown. —   Rock-in' in the U. S. A. —

1.
E   A   D   A   E   A   D   A

2. Well, they

2.
E   A   D   E   A   D

Recorder Solo
E   A   D   A *play 4 times*

Guitar Solo
E   A   D   A *play 4 times*   E   (drums & organ)   *D.S. al Coda*   **3**

⊕ **Coda**
E   A   D   A   N.C.

Outro-Chorus
E   A   D   A

R.   O.   C.   K.   in   the   U.   S.   A. ———   R. —

Repeat and fade
E   A   D   A

— O.   C.   K.   in   the   U.   S.   A. ———   R. —

I'M YOURS

Words and Music by
Jason Mraz

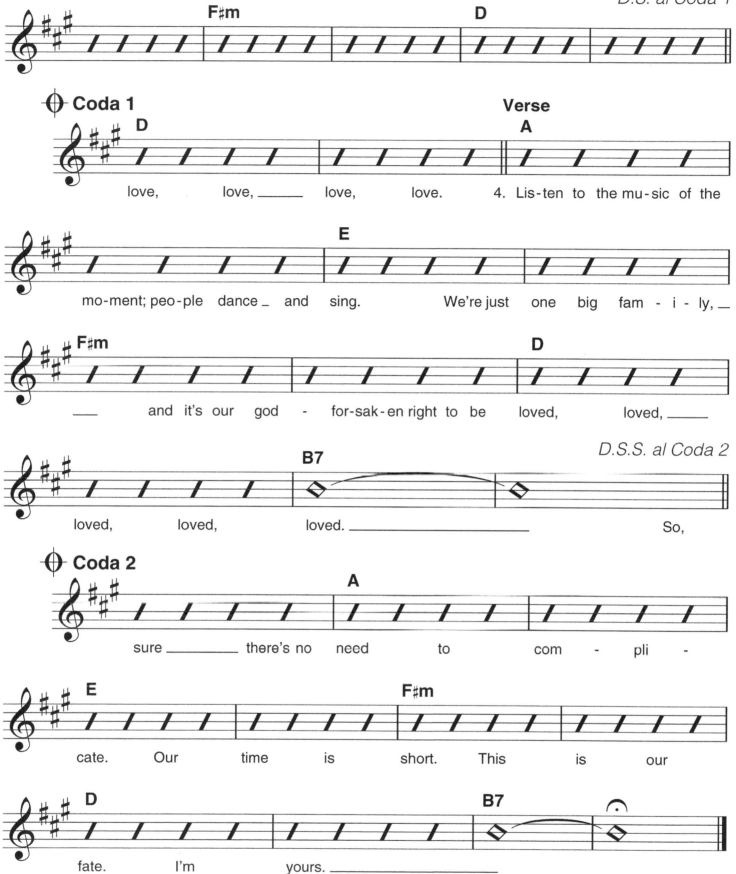

Coda 1

Verse

love, love, _____ love, love. 4. Lis-ten to the mu-sic of the

mo-ment; peo-ple dance _ and sing. We're just one big fam - i - ly, _

_ and it's our god - for-sak-en right to be loved, loved, _____

D.S.S. al Coda 2

loved, loved, loved. _____ So,

Coda 2

sure _____ there's no need to com - pli -

cate. Our time is short. This is our

fate. I'm yours. _____

Additional Lyrics

3. Well, open up your mind and see like me.
   Open up your plans and, damn, you're free.
   Look into your heart and you'll find
   Love, love, love, love.

UPSIDE DOWN
from the Universal Pictures and Imagine Entertainment film
CURIOUS GEORGE

Words and Music by
Jack Johnson

Additional Lyrics

3. Who's to say
I can't do ev'rything? Well, I can try.
And as I roll along, I begin to find
Things aren't always just what they seem.

CRAZY LITTLE THING CALLED LOVE

Words and Music by
Freddie Mercury

ACROSS THE UNIVERSE

Words and Music by
John Lennon and Paul McCartney

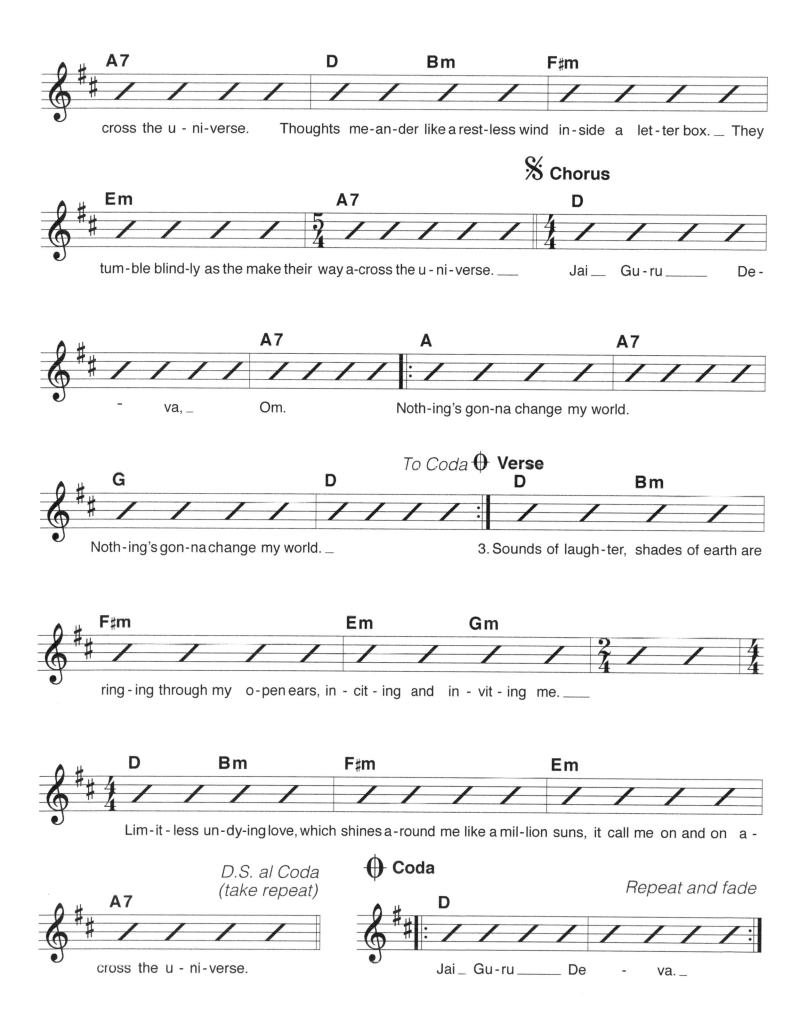

I WILL

Words and Music by
John Lennon and Paul McCartney

Love you when-ev-er we're____ to-geth-er, love you when we're_ a - part._

Verse

____ 3. And when_____ at last_ I find___ you, your song_

____ will fill___ the air. ____ Sing it loud___ so I___ can hear_

___ you, make it eas - y to ___ be near ___ you, for the things_

____ you do ___ en-dear ___ you to ___ me. Ah, _____ you know ___ I will. _

____ I will. _____

Outro

Mm, _____ mm. _____ Da, da, da, _ da, la, la. _

SMOOTH

Words by Rob Thomas
Music by Rob Thomas and Itaal Shur

E7 / / / | Am / F / | E7 / / / |

lift   you up.   I could change   my   life   to   bet-ter   suit __ your __ mood __

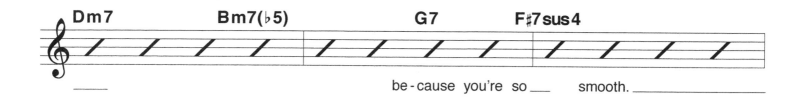

Dm7 / / / | Bm7(♭5) / / | G7 / F♯7sus4 / |

__   be-cause you're so __   smooth. _____

Chorus

E7 / / / | Am / F / | E7 / / / |

__   Well, and it's   just like the o - cean   un-der the moon. Well, it's the

Am / F / | E7 / / / | Am / F / |

same as the e-mo-tion that I   get from   you. __   You   got the kind of lov-in' that can

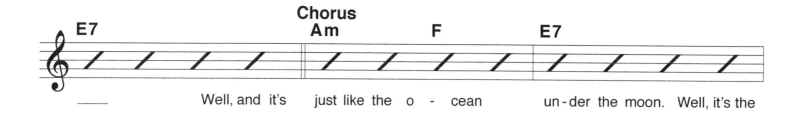

E7 / / / | Dm7 / / | E7 / / |

be   so   smooth, __ yeah.   Gim-me   your heart, __   make   it   real.

1. **Interlude**

N.C. — | Am / F / | E7 / / / |

Or else for-get a-bout it.

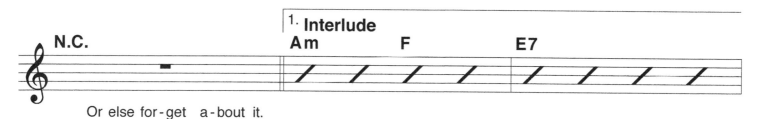

D.S. (take repeat) | 2.

Am / F / | E7 / / / | (drums)

3. Well, I'll   tell   you

Guitar Solo

Chorus

And it's   just like the o - cean

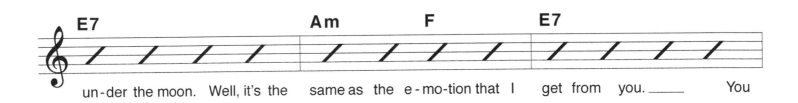

un-der the moon. Well, it's the   same as the e -mo-tion that I   get from you._____   You

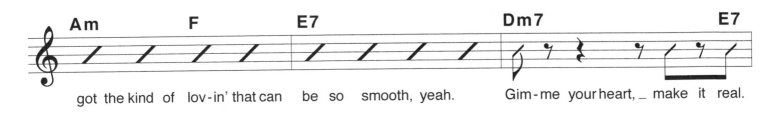

got the kind of lov-in' that can   be so   smooth, yeah.   Gim-me your heart, _ make it real.

Outro   *Repeat and fade*

Or else for-get a-bout it.   Let's all for-get a-bout it.

WHILE MY GUITAR GENTLY WEEPS

Words and Music by
George Harrison

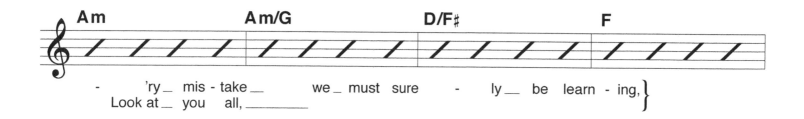

'ry _ mis - take _ we _ must sure - ly _ be learn - ing,
Look at _ you all, _____

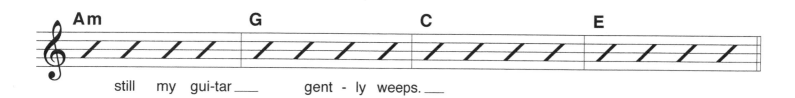

still my gui-tar ___ gent - ly weeps. ___

Guitar Solo

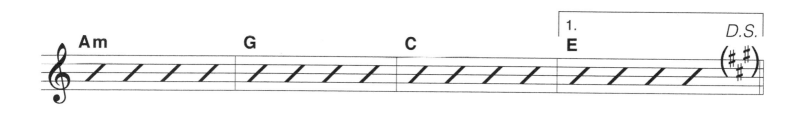

STRUM PATTERNS

The first responsibility of a chord player is to *play the right chord on time*. Keep this in mind as you learn new strumming patterns. No matter how concerned you might be with right-hand strumming, getting to the correct chord with your left hand is more important. If necessary, leave the old chord early in order to arrive at the new chord on time.

That said, here are some suggested strum patterns. Choose one that challenges you, and practice it. Whenever you learn a new chord or progression, try putting it into one of these patterns. Also, try applying these to the songs in this book.

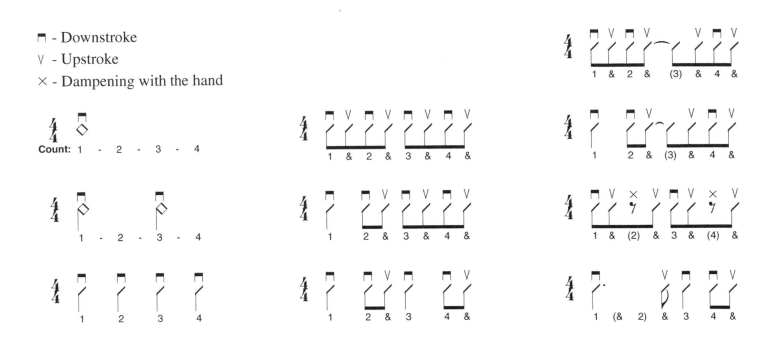

Eighth notes in the above strums may be played even or uneven ("swung") depending on the style of music.

46

HAL LEONARD GUITAR METHOD

METHOD BOOKS, SONGBOOKS AND REFERENCE BOOKS

THE HAL LEONARD GUITAR METHOD is designed for anyone just learning to play acoustic or electric guitar. It is based on years of teaching guitar students of all ages, and it also reflects some of the best guitar teaching ideas from around the world. This comprehensive method includes: A learning sequence carefully paced with clear instructions; popular songs which increase the incentive to learn to play; versatility – can be used as self-instruction or with a teacher; audio accompaniments so that students have fun and sound great while practicing.

BOOK 1
00699010	Book Only	$8.99
00699027	Book/Online Audio	$12.99
00697341	Book/Online Audio + DVD	$24.99
00697318	DVD Only	$19.99
00155480	Deluxe Beginner Edition (Book, CD, DVD, Online Audio/ Video & Chord Poster)	$19.99

COMPLETE (BOOKS 1, 2 & 3)
00699040	Book Only	$16.99
00697342	Book/Online Audio	$24.99

BOOK 2
00699020	Book Only	$8.99
00697313	Book/Online Audio	$12.99

BOOK 3
00699030	Book Only	$8.99
00697316	Book/Online Audio	$12.99

Prices, contents and availability subject to change without notice.

STYLISTIC METHODS

ACOUSTIC GUITAR
00697347	Method Book/Online Audio	$17.99
00237969	Songbook/Online Audio	$16.99

BLUEGRASS GUITAR
00697405	Method Book/Online Audio	$16.99

BLUES GUITAR
00697326	Method Book/Online Audio (9" x 12")	$16.99
00697344	Method Book/Online Audio (6" x 9")	$15.99
00697385	Songbook/Online Audio (9" x 12")	$14.99
00248636	Kids Method Book/Online Audio	$12.99

BRAZILIAN GUITAR
00697415	Method Book/Online Audio	$17.99

CHRISTIAN GUITAR
00695947	Method Book/Online Audio	$16.99
00697408	Songbook/CD Pack	$14.99

CLASSICAL GUITAR
00697376	Method Book/Online Audio	$15.99

COUNTRY GUITAR
00697337	Method Book/Online Audio	$22.99
00697400	Songbook/Online Audio	$19.99

FINGERSTYLE GUITAR
00697378	Method Book/Online Audio	$21.99
00697432	Songbook/Online Audio	$16.99

FLAMENCO GUITAR
00697363	Method Book/Online Audio	$15.99

FOLK GUITAR
00697414	Method Book/Online Audio	$16.99

JAZZ GUITAR
00695359	Book/Online Audio	$22.99
00697386	Songbook/Online Audio	$15.99

JAZZ-ROCK FUSION
00697387	Book/Online Audio	$24.99

R&B GUITAR
00697356	Book/Online Audio	$19.99
00697433	Songbook/CD Pack	$14.99

ROCK GUITAR
00697319	Book/Online Audio	$16.99
00697383	Songbook/Online Audio	$16.99

ROCKABILLY GUITAR
00697407	Book/Online Audio	$16.99

OTHER METHOD BOOKS

BARITONE GUITAR METHOD
00242055	Book/Online Audio	$12.99

GUITAR FOR KIDS
00865003	Method Book 1/Online Audio	$12.99
00697402	Songbook/Online Audio	$9.99
00128437	Method Book 2/Online Audio	$12.99

MUSIC THEORY FOR GUITARISTS
00695790	Book/Online Audio	$19.99

TENOR GUITAR METHOD
00148330	Book/Online Audio	$12.99

12-STRING GUITAR METHOD
00249528	Book/Online Audio	$19.99

METHOD SUPPLEMENTS

ARPEGGIO FINDER
00697352	6" x 9" Edition	$6.99
00697351	9" x 12" Edition	$9.99

BARRE CHORDS
00697406	Book/Online Audio	$14.99

CHORD, SCALE & ARPEGGIO FINDER
00697410	Book Only	$19.99

GUITAR TECHNIQUES
00697389	Book/Online Audio	$16.99

INCREDIBLE CHORD FINDER
00697200	6" x 9" Edition	$7.99
00697208	9" x 12" Edition	$7.99

INCREDIBLE SCALE FINDER
00695568	6" x 9" Edition	$9.99
00695490	9" x 12" Edition	$9.99

LEAD LICKS
00697345	Book/Online Audio	$10.99

RHYTHM RIFFS
00697346	Book/Online Audio	$14.99

SONGBOOKS

CLASSICAL GUITAR PIECES
00697388	Book/Online Audio	$9.99

EASY POP MELODIES
00697281	Book Only	$7.99
00697440	Book/Online Audio	$14.99

(MORE) EASY POP MELODIES
00697280	Book Only	$6.99
00697269	Book/Online Audio	$14.99

(EVEN MORE) EASY POP MELODIES
00699154	Book Only	$6.99
00697439	Book/Online Audio	$14.99

EASY POP RHYTHMS
00697336	Book Only	$7.99
00697441	Book/Online Audio	$14.99

(MORE) EASY POP RHYTHMS
00697338	Book Only	$7.99
00697322	Book/Online Audio	$14.99

(EVEN MORE) EASY POP RHYTHMS
00697340	Book Only	$7.99
00697323	Book/Online Audio	$14.99

EASY POP CHRISTMAS MELODIES
00697417	Book Only	$9.99
00697416	Book/Online Audio	$14.99

EASY POP CHRISTMAS RHYTHMS
00278177	Book Only	$6.99
00278175	Book/Online Audio	$14.99

EASY SOLO GUITAR PIECES
00110407	Book Only	$9.99

REFERENCE

GUITAR PRACTICE PLANNER
00697401	Book Only	$5.99

GUITAR SETUP & MAINTENANCE
00697427	6" x 9" Edition	$14.99
00697421	9" x 12" Edition	$12.99

For more info, songlists, or to purchase these and more books from your favorite music retailer, go to

halleonard.com

HAL•LEONARD®

EASY GUITAR WITH NOTES & TAB

This series features simplified arrangements with notes, tab, chord charts, and strum and pick patterns.

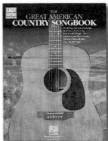

MIXED FOLIOS

00702287	Acoustic	$19.99
00702002	Acoustic Rock Hits for Easy Guitar	$15.99
00702166	All-Time Best Guitar Collection	$19.99
00702232	Best Acoustic Songs for Easy Guitar	$16.99
00119835	Best Children's Songs	$16.99
00703055	The Big Book of Nursery Rhymes & Children's Songs	$16.99
00698978	Big Christmas Collection	$19.99
00702394	Bluegrass Songs for Easy Guitar	$15.99
00289632	Bohemian Rhapsody	$19.99
00703387	Celtic Classics	$14.99
00224808	Chart Hits of 2016-2017	$14.99
00267383	Chart Hits of 2017-2018	$14.99
00334293	Chart Hits of 2019-2020	$16.99
00702149	Children's Christian Songbook	$9.99
00702028	Christmas Classics	$8.99
00101779	Christmas Guitar	$14.99
00702141	Classic Rock	$8.95
00159642	Classical Melodies	$12.99
00253933	Disney/Pixar's Coco	$16.99
00702203	CMT's 100 Greatest Country Songs	$34.99
00702283	The Contemporary Christian Collection	$16.99
00196954	Contemporary Disney	$19.99
00702239	Country Classics for Easy Guitar	$24.99

00702257	Easy Acoustic Guitar Songs	$16.99
00702041	Favorite Hymns for Easy Guitar	$12.99
00222701	Folk Pop Songs	$17.99
00126894	Frozen	$14.99
00333922	Frozen 2	$14.99
00702286	Glee	$16.99
00702160	The Great American Country Songbook	$19.99
00702148	Great American Gospel for Guitar	$14.99
00702050	Great Classical Themes for Easy Guitar	$9.99
00275088	The Greatest Showman	$17.99
00148030	Halloween Guitar Songs	$14.99
00702273	Irish Songs	$12.99
00192503	Jazz Classics for Easy Guitar	$16.99
00702275	Jazz Favorites for Easy Guitar	$17.99
00702274	Jazz Standards for Easy Guitar	$19.99
00702162	Jumbo Easy Guitar Songbook	$24.99
00232285	La La Land	$16.99
00702258	Legends of Rock	$14.99
00702189	MTV's 100 Greatest Pop Songs	$34.99
00702272	1950s Rock	$16.99
00702271	1960s Rock	$16.99
00702270	1970s Rock	$19.99
00702269	1980s Rock	$15.99
00702268	1990s Rock	$19.99
00369043	Rock Songs for Kids	$14.99

00109725	Once	$14.99
00702187	Selections from O Brother Where Art Thou?	$19.99
00702178	100 Songs for Kids	$14.99
00702515	Pirates of the Caribbean	$17.99
00702125	Praise and Worship for Guitar	$14.99
00287930	Songs from *A Star Is Born, The Greatest Showman, La La Land*, and More Movie Musicals	$16.99
00702285	Southern Rock Hits	$12.99
00156420	Star Wars Music	$16.99
00121535	30 Easy Celtic Guitar Solos	$16.99
00702156	3-Chord Rock	$12.99
00244654	Top Hits of 2017	$14.99
00283786	Top Hits of 2018	$14.99
00702294	Top Worship Hits	$17.99
00702255	VH1's 100 Greatest Hard Rock Songs	$34.99
00702175	VH1's 100 Greatest Songs of Rock and Roll	$29.99
00702253	Wicked	$12.99

ARTIST COLLECTIONS

00702267	AC/DC for Easy Guitar	$16.99
00702598	Adele for Easy Guitar	$15.99
00156221	Adele – 25	$16.99
00702040	Best of the Allman Brothers	$16.99
00702865	J.S. Bach for Easy Guitar	$15.99
00702169	Best of The Beach Boys	$15.99
00702292	The Beatles — 1	$22.99
00125796	Best of Chuck Berry	$15.99
00702201	The Essential Black Sabbath	$15.99
00702250	blink-182 — Greatest Hits	$17.99
02501615	Zac Brown Band — The Foundation	$17.99
02501621	Zac Brown Band — You Get What You Give	$16.99
00702043	Best of Johnny Cash	$17.99
00702090	Eric Clapton's Best	$16.99
00702086	Eric Clapton — from the Album Unplugged	$17.99
00702202	The Essential Eric Clapton	$17.99
00702053	Best of Patsy Cline	$15.99
00222697	Very Best of Coldplay – 2nd Edition	$16.99
00702229	The Very Best of Creedence Clearwater Revival	$16.99
00702145	Best of Jim Croce	$16.99
00702278	Crosby, Stills & Nash	$12.99
14042809	Bob Dylan	$15.99
00702276	Fleetwood Mac — Easy Guitar Collection	$17.99
00139462	The Very Best of Grateful Dead	$16.99
00702136	Best of Merle Haggard	$16.99
00702227	Jimi Hendrix — Smash Hits	$19.99
00702288	Best of Hillsong United	$12.99
00702236	Best of Antonio Carlos Jobim	$15.99
00702245	Elton John — Greatest Hits 1970–2002	$19.99

00129855	Jack Johnson	$16.99
00702204	Robert Johnson	$14.99
00702234	Selections from Toby Keith — 35 Biggest Hits	$12.95
00702003	Kiss	$16.99
00702216	Lynyrd Skynyrd	$16.99
00702182	The Essential Bob Marley	$16.99
00146081	Maroon 5	$14.99
00121925	Bruno Mars – Unorthodox Jukebox	$12.99
00702248	Paul McCartney — All the Best	$14.99
00125484	The Best of MercyMe	$12.99
00702209	Steve Miller Band — Young Hearts (Greatest Hits)	$12.95
00124167	Jason Mraz	$15.99
00702096	Best of Nirvana	$16.99
00702211	The Offspring — Greatest Hits	$17.99
00138026	One Direction	$17.99
00702030	Best of Roy Orbison	$17.99
00702144	Best of Ozzy Osbourne	$14.99
00702279	Tom Petty	$17.99
00102911	Pink Floyd	$17.99
00702139	Elvis Country Favorites	$19.99
00702293	The Very Best of Prince	$19.99
00699415	Best of Queen for Guitar	$16.99
00109279	Best of R.E.M.	$14.99
00702208	Red Hot Chili Peppers — Greatest Hits	$16.99
00198960	The Rolling Stones	$17.99
00174793	The Very Best of Santana	$16.99
00702196	Best of Bob Seger	$16.99
00146046	Ed Sheeran	$15.99
00702252	Frank Sinatra — Nothing But the Best	$12.99
00702010	Best of Rod Stewart	$17.99
00702049	Best of George Strait	$17.99

00702259	Taylor Swift for Easy Guitar	$15.99
00359800	Taylor Swift – Easy Guitar Anthology	$24.99
00702260	Taylor Swift — Fearless	$14.99
00139727	Taylor Swift — 1989	$17.99
00115960	Taylor Swift — Red	$16.99
00253667	Taylor Swift — Reputation	$17.99
00702290	Taylor Swift — Speak Now	$16.99
00232849	Chris Tomlin Collection – 2nd Edition	$14.99
00702226	Chris Tomlin — See the Morning	$12.95
00148643	Train	$14.99
00702427	U2 — 18 Singles	$19.99
00702108	Best of Stevie Ray Vaughan	$17.99
00279005	The Who	$14.99
00702123	Best of Hank Williams	$15.99
00194548	Best of John Williams	$14.99
00702228	Neil Young — Greatest Hits	$17.99
00119133	Neil Young — Harvest	$14.99

Prices, contents and availability subject to change without notice.

Visit Hal Leonard online at **halleonard.com**